W9-BVH-892

Bride's · Little · Book · of

BOUQUETS
and
FLOWERS

CLARKSON N. POTTER / PUBLISHERS, NEW YORK

acknowledgments

BRIDE'S especially wants to thank MARIA McBRIDE-MELLINGER, Contributing Editor, for her innovative vision in the area of floral styling. Thanks, too, to RACHEL LEONARD, Fashion Editor, for her creative editorial concepts. Bouquets to ANDREA FELD, Managing Editor, for her fresh insights on beautifying the style of the text, and for keeping the project on track. And cascades of thanks to ROCHELLE UDELL and MARY MAGUIRE of The Condé Nast Publications Inc. for making this book happen, to LAUREN SHAKELY of Clarkson N. Potter, and to BRIDE'S Art Director PHYLLIS RICHMOND COX. Thanks to Kathy Mullins, the book's writer/researcher. And appreciation to BRIDE'S staff members Wendy Caisse Curran, Ashley Thompson, and Wendy Marder, for handling copy editing, photographers' permissions, and fact checking, respectively. And, a very special thank-you to the talented florists and professionals whose work appears in this book.

Florists: Christopher Bassett (pg. 27); L. Becker Flowers (pg. 29); Blue Meadow Flowers (pg. 14); Leslie Ferrar Designs (pgs. 34, 35); Fresh Art (pg. 36); Curtis Godwin (pgs. 8; 12; 26, top; 30); Pure Madderlake (pg. 28); Alexandra Randall Flowers (pgs. 15; 26, bottom; 39; 41); Renny (both photos, pg. 38); Twigs (pg. 33); Bobby Wiggins (pgs. 7; 10; 16-17; 18-19; 20-21; 22-23; 24; 25; 31; 32; 40, both photos; 42; 43; 44).

Photographers: Calliope (pg. 41); Walter Chin (pgs. 42, 44); Michael Geiger (pgs. 28, 33); Oberto Gili (pgs. 29, 30, 31); Guzman (pgs. 34, 35, 36); Connie Hansen (pgs. 18-19; 20-21; 22-23); Gabriella Imperatori (cover, pg. 25); Douglas Keeve (pg. 12); Christopher Micaud (pgs. 4, 7, 10); Kei Ogata (pg. 38, both photos); Lilo Raymond (pgs. 15; 26, top); Maria Robledo (pgs. 16-17; 24; 26, bottom; 27; 32; 40, both photos); Karl Stoecker (pg. 43, all photos); Bico Stupakoff (pg. 39); William Waldron (pgs. 8, 14).

Copyright © 1993 by The Condé Nast Publications Inc. All rights reserved. No part of this book may be reproduced or transmitted in any form or by any means, electronic or mechanical, including photocopying recording, or by any information storage and retrieval stystem, without permission in writing from the publisher.

Published by Clarkson N. Potter, Inc. 201 East 50th Street, New York, New York 10022. Member of the Crown Publishing Group. CLARKSON N. POTTER, POTTER and colophon are trademarks of Clarkson N. Potter, Inc. Manufactured in Hong Kong.

Design by Justine Strasberg

Library of Congress Cataloging-in-Publication Data
Bride's little book of flowers / by the editors of Bride's magazine.
    p.   cm.
1. Bridal bouquets.   I. Bride's (The Condé Nast Publications Inc.)
2. Title: Little book of flowers.
SB449.5.B7B75   1993
745.92'6 — dc20   92-23644
                                                    CIP

ISBN 0-517-59295-9
10 9 8 7 6 5

contents

introduction

"He sent her flowers after their first date"... "Their love flowered with each passing day"... "Finally, he proposed in the most romantic, flowery way"... The language of flowers—whether noun, verb, or adjective—is symbolic of every aspect of love and romance. From the heraldry of the fleur-de-lis to simpler symbols of love (red rose), purity (lily of the valley), chastity (orange blossom), fidelity (ivy), flowers speak volumes. This small volume of floral lore is designed to inspire every bride and groom as they select flowers for their wedding day: fragrant white blooms at the altar, a daisy chain to mark the pews, fantasy bouquets for the bride and her attendants, tulips on the reception tables. Even the petals tossed by the flower girl are replete with meaning. As the most loving gesture of all, a bride plucks a spray of blossoms from the center of her bouquet and pins it to her groom's lapel at the altar... her floral tribute to his love and to a lifetime of sharing.

BARBARA TOBER

Editor-in-Chief, BRIDE'S magazine

Flowers have long symbolized love and joy. The bride's bouquet—fragrant, enchanting—heralds joy and a future ripe with abundant possibilities. Centuries ago, instead of flowers, English brides carried aromatic herbs, such as sage, thyme, and garlic, to ward off evil spirits who might interfere with nuptial happiness. In Tudor England, sprigs from bouquets of herbs and flowers with assumed aphrodisiac powers (for example, dill, marigolds dipped in rosewater) were even eaten by brides!

the history of the bouquet

At the beginning of the twentieth century, extravagant bouquets sometimes measured two feet across and trailed ribbons knotted with tiny flower heads. Sophisticated brides in the twenties carried sleek sheaves of calla lilies or a simple "posy" of bright nasturtiums or orchids. During the early thirties, brides carried abundant armfuls of blossoms—gladioli, stock, and lilies. Toward the decade's end, simplicity reigned—in pretty Victorian posies of azaleas, violets, and pansies. During World War II, when flowers were scarce, brides carried simple, fragrant nosegays of lilies of the valley, roses, and gardenias. The flower-child bride of the early seventies gathered fresh wildflowers for a natural bouquet. And in the opulent eighties, floral designers treated the bouquet as

an art form, weaving unusual imported blooms, gilded fruits, lace, and gorgeous ribbon into lavish arrangements. Today, bridal flowers may be fashion statements—boas, necklaces, bracelets, pocket adornments, hair accessories—coordinating with the color and texture of the gown fabric.

The ceremonial tossing of the bridal bouquet is a symbolic moment. The bride gathers the single women in attendance and throws her bouquet (or a smaller, less-expensive replica) as a token of good luck. The lucky maiden who catches it will supposedly be the next to marry. Bridesmaids in England today still pluck a sprig (usually of myrtle, a lucky flower that portends harmony) from the bride's bouquet and plant it beside the entry of the newlyweds' home.

> *Roses arranged as precisely as petals in a single bloom.*

BOUQUET BASICS

working with your florist

Ask friends for florist recommendations; evaluate store displays for freshness, creativity. Three months before the wedding, make an appointment; take along fabric and linen swatches, names of flowers preferred, pictures of gowns; outline floral budget, special needs (for example, pew markers). Bouquets should complement gowns, be scaled to body proportions. Florist and customer should both sign a contract listing flower types, colors; substitutes (if necessary); numbers and sizes of arrangements and bouquets; date, time, of wedding; addresses; deposit, amount of balance and date due.

flowers for all seasons

Here, flowers in bloom for spring and summer weddings.

· ·

PICTURED, RIGHT:
1] CAMELLIA (WITH FOLIAGE);
2] RANUNCULUS; 3] SWEET PEA;
4] TULIP, "APRICOT BEAUTY";
5] LILAC (LAVENDER);
6] VIBURNUM; 7] ROSE, "SERENA";
8] TULIP, "ANGELIQUE"; 9] SPRAY
ROSE, "EVELIENE"; 10] TULIP,
"DREAMLAND"; 11] SPRAY ROSE,
"PINK DELIGHT"; 12] BLUE LACE
FLOWER; 13] ITALIAN HYACINTH;
14] ANEMONE; 15] TULIP,
"APRICOT PARROT"; 16] ITALIAN
CARNATION, "EOLO";
17] NARCISSUS, "CRAGFORD";
18] ROSE, "WHITE BUTTERFLY."
OTHER OPTIONS: DAFFODILS,
DAHLIAS, JASMINE, PANSIES,
PEONIES, "SHASTA" DAISIES.

SPRING/SUMMER

Most flowers are fuller, hardier, available in more variety, and less expensive during their peak growing time. Vibrant hues warm the senses when the weather turns cool, add excitement to the procession.

. . . .

PICTURED, RIGHT:
1] PARROT TULIP, "FLAME";
2] STOCK; 3] ICELAND POPPY;
4] CALLA LILY;
5] GLORIOSA LILY; 6] LILAC;
7] CALENDULA; 8] HYBRID
NERINE; 9] VIOLET;
10] ROSE, "GRETA";
11] CYCLAMEN;
12] BACHELOR'S BUTTON;
13] BOUVARDIA;
14] RANUNCULUS;
15] FLORIDA HOLLY;
16] ILEX; 17] VARIEGATED IVY.
OTHER OPTIONS: AMARYLLIS,
HEATHER, HOLLY, MIMOSA,
SUNFLOWERS.

FALL/WINTER

ALL YEAR

f your heart is set on a particular flower, most can be imported or ordered anytime from hothouses. Some flowers blossom year-round in many climates. Roses are abundant in June and in December—both popular months for weddings.

. . . .

PICTURED, LEFT:

1] EASTER LILY, "LONGIFLORUM";
2] TUBEROSE; 3] CALLA LILY;
4] PHALAENOPSIS ORCHID;
5] MAIDENHAIR FERN;
6] ROSE, "WHITE BUTTERFLY";
7] LILY OF THE VALLEY;
8] STOCK;
9] CATTLEYA ORCHID;
10] CASABLANCA LILY;
11] STEPHANOTIS;
12] QUEEN ANNE'S LACE;
13] GARDENIA;
14] VARIEGATED IVY.

OTHER OPTIONS: ALSTROEMERIA, BABY'S BREATH, FREESIA, IRIS, BELLS OF IRELAND.

Ever since Queen Victoria wed in white in 1840, white has remained traditional for wedding gowns and bouquets. All white and cream bouquets have become symbolic of the qualities of purity and serenity. Classic and elegant, the white bouquet looks even better by candlelight — at "after-five" ceremonies. The all-white bouquet might be a cascade of orange blossoms, roses, violets, camellias, lilac; a posy of white stock, lilies of the valley, peonies, astrantia, and freesia wired loosely;

classic white bouquets

or an abundantly lush nosegay of stephanotis and hyacinth (left). Use just one or two varieties for a more formal bouquet. To weave rich texture, subtle patterns, mingle intensities of white; pair just-picked rosebuds with full bloomers and past-peak roses, tiny snowdrops with pouffy peonies. Introduce whispers of color... a sprinkling of Stargazing Lilies with deep-red centers stand out among traditional bridal whites.

Mix white and near-white flowers, now available year-round; techniques for conditioning and manipulating exotic blooms are also being perfected. Dendrobium orchids, wild sweet peas, jasmine, "Serena" roses and other favorite whites (in ivory, champagne, ecru, creamy white, and pure white) create unusual bouquets. Fragile sprigs of apple blossom pair with palest blush tulips, fair peonies, white lilacs.

modern white bouquets

Petals and small blossoms, layered inside each other, create one large composite faux bloom. Clusters of small

flowers, crafted together, form a single generous blossom, mounted on a gilded or ribbon-braided solitary stem. Bold strokes of foliage (e.g., the gilded leaves, right) add sculptural detail.

bouquet styles

[THE BIEDERMEIER]

→ *Small nosegay with concentric rings of alternating blooms.*

Here, floral options to wear or carry — fashion accents that complement the personality of the bride and her gown.

[P O M A N D E R]

Blossom-covered globe carried from a satin ribbon.

*Cluster of individual blooms (here, gladiola florets) comprise
one fantasy flower on a single stem.*

[THE CASCADE]

*Graceful spill of blossoms, greenery, and ribbon flowing
downward from the bouquet's base, along front of gown.*

[PENDANT]

 *Fragrant, fresh "Serena" roses and hyacinths arranged
into a wearable, heart-shaped, beribboned locket.*

[HANDTIED]

→ *Blooms loosely arranged and wrapped with a ribbon,
piece of tulle or satin, leaves or bark.*

beyond the bouquet

[HAT BAND] → *Lavish cascade of blossoms sewn to hat brim.*

[B O A] › *Luxurious garland of wired flowers worn as a stole.*

[POCKET POSY] ⟩ *Chic, sophisticated clutch of blooms.*

cost-saving tips

Within any budget, grand or sparse, an imaginative florist can create exquisite bridal bouquets and floral accessories. Set your spending limit first, then, if necessary, talk to the florist about getting the look you want with cost-saving substitutes. Select in-season, locally grown flowers—more plentiful and less expensive. Don't schedule a wedding on the weekend of a flower-giving holiday (e.g., near Mother's Day, Valentine's Day); blooms are pricier. Avoid labor-intensive, large, handwired bouquets—the most costly alternative. Opt for handtied bouquets with fewer blossoms. Scout antique stores for lace, tulle, ribbon, pearls; give them to your florist to weave into bouquets. Have bridesmaids carry one dramatic stem. Arrange a single mass of baby's breath—it's lush, more affordable. Select an ornate wedding location needing less decoration.

bridesmaids' bouquets

The shape and style of bridesmaids' flowers should complement the bridal bouquet and flatter each attendant's stature. Maids' bouquets can be baskets filled with sunburst hues (right) that echo the floral motif of garden-print dresses—apricot roses, deep-coral ranunculus, and golden tulips. For different jewel-tone gowns, select Dutch Tulips, in contrasting colors, tied with moiré ribbons. Like the bride, attendants may wear flowers as hair accessories, hat trim, necklaces, bracelets, or pendants pinned to gowns. For a Victorian wedding, have maids carry tussie-mussies—tightly packed nosegays of flowers, herbs, and foliage in silver posy holders.

flowers for children

A necklace of dainty blossoms leaves small hands free to scatter rose petals. Blooms may be worn as hair wreaths, headbands, or bracelets, or nestled into sashes for littlest misses. Ring bearers may tuck pocket posies into jacket pockets. Most-charming wedding nosegays have soft colors,

diminutive blossoms, and gorgeous ribbon streamers. Other pretty and manageable choices: a floral ball or pomander to loop around a tiny arm; whimsical flower hoops or garlands of greenery and flowers—a popular choice for the children in recent English royal weddings. Garlands are finished with pretty bows that form carrying handles, and may be used to hang garlands at the altar as decorations during the wedding ceremony.

The traditional white carnation or rosebud are just two boutonniere options. Any flower small in scale— bud, tiny floret backed with baby's breath or foliage—is a possibility. The groom often chooses flowers in the bride's bouquet; his boutonniere may be a "pull-away" concealed in her arrangement; (she then pins it to his lapel

boutonnieres: a groom's bloom

at the altar). Classic blooms for groomsmen: stephanotis or a sprig of freesia with greenery. More unusual options: (Left) a gloriosa lily. (Above, left to right) ranunculus, a calla lily, and phlox. Or, consider a scaled-down sunflower, a bachelor's button, grape hyacinth, and narcissus. Pin boutonnieres on left lapels.

Flowers speak the language of romance through hidden meanings. Send your groom a subtle message in your bouquet: red tulips (declaration of love), ivy (fidelity), white roses ("you're heavenly"), or lilacs (first emotions of love). Or, spell his name, a message, with flowers: jasmine, ivy, magnolias, tell J-I-M he's special; lilies of the valley, orchids, violets, everlasting, send a message of L-O-V-E.

fragrant messages

Tell bridesmaids you're honored by their presence by including a special message in each bouquet. Pansies, white clover, forget-me-nots ("ours is a special friendship"); blue violets (loyalty, faithfulness); or blue periwinkle (early friendship) are all ways to say "I'm glad you're you."

Thank-yous to parents come in pretty possibilities: white bellflowers (for gratitude); baskets of colorful pansies ("you are in my thoughts").

Particularly aromatic flowers, perfect for potpourri: daffodils, freesia, gardenias, grape hyacinths, irises, jasmine, lilacs, lilies, magnolia, roses, stephanotis, violets.